W9-CRG-159

CALGARY PUBLIC LIBRARY

SEA
TURTLES

SEA
TURTLES

DON PATTON
THE CHILD'S WORLD

The sea turtle glides gracefully over the coral reef. Like an eagle soaring through the sky, the turtle flies through the water using powerful strokes of her flippers. Under the cover of darkness she turns toward shore, moving closer to the beach. The water is only inches deep now, and the flippers that serve her so well for swimming are not well adapted for life on land. She drags herself up the beach, the strong instinct to lay her eggs pushing her further and further up the sloping sand. The difference between her graceful swim and her awkward struggle across the beach makes it obvious that she is truly a creature of the sea.

Unlike pond and land turtles, and tortoises, the sea turtle has adapted to life in the oceans. The powerful legs common on tortoises have been adapted into large, blade-shaped flippers for the sea turtle. The heavy shell seen on most turtles is lightweight and streamlined, making it easier for the turtle to push itself through the water. The smaller shell keeps the sea turtle from pulling into its shell as other turtles do when they are threatened.

There are eight species of sea turtles in the world, all of them threatened with extinction. They range in size from the small *olive ridley* and *Kemp's ridley* (with shells 30 inches long) to the huge *leatherback* (74 inches long). A full-grown adult leatherback can weigh more than 2,000 pounds! Sea turtles can live to be fifty to sixty years old.

Sea turtles are found in the Mediterranean Sea, the Gulf of Mexico, and most of the warm oceans of the world. The leatherback has even adapted to living in the cold waters of the Arctic for a portion of the year.

Many sea turtles migrate long distances during their lifetimes. The *green sea turtle* migrates 2,800 miles from the coast of Brazil to lay its eggs on the predator-free beaches of Ascension Island, in the mid-Atlantic. A beach where large numbers of females gather to lay eggs is called a *rookery*. In its migration to and from the rookeries, the giant leatherback turtle travels over 5,000 miles a year!

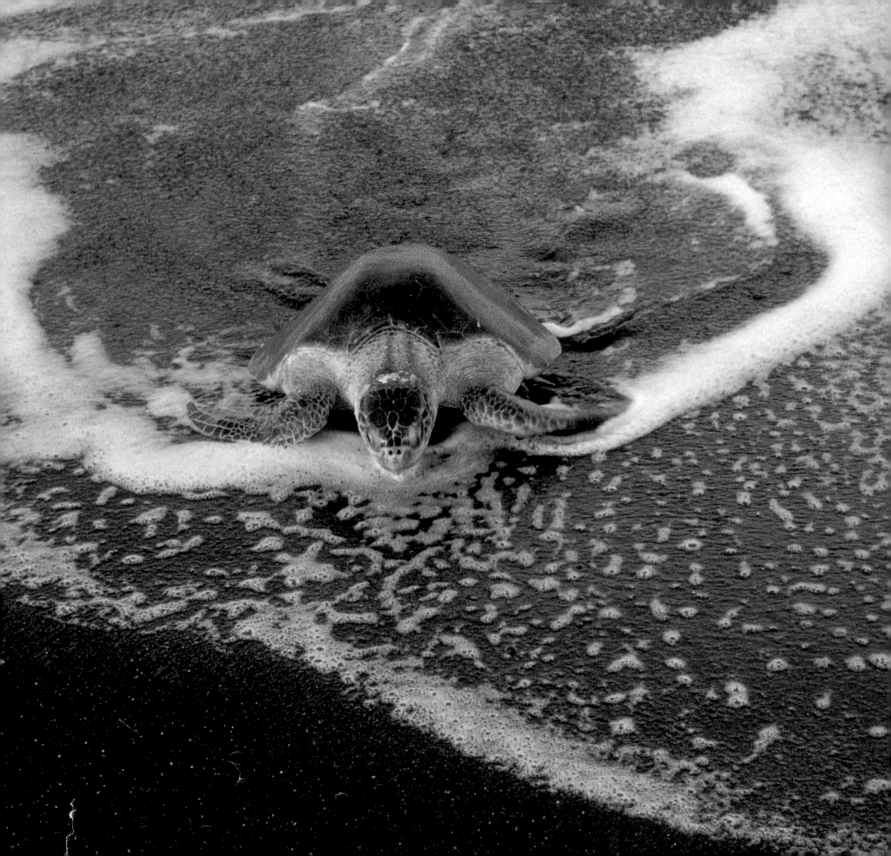

Sea turtles feed on a variety of plants and animals. Baby turtles feed on small shrimp, jellyfish, algae, and insects blown from shore. Adult turtles are picky about what they eat. Adult green turtles like to eat a sea grass commonly found in shallow, sandy areas. Seabirds are often seen perched on the backs of olive ridley turtles as the turtles ride the waves in the open ocean, feeding on small shrimp. An oily layer of insulation in its skin helps the huge leatherback dive into the cold ocean depths, 3,000 feet down, to feed on big jellyfish. Since sea turtles are air-breathing animals, they must return to the surface for air. Nevertheless, some sea turtles can spend as long as five hours underwater between breaths!

Sea turtles mate during spring and summer. The male sea turtle has a long tail that it uses to hold onto the female during mating. The eggs develop inside the female for two to two and a half months before they are ready to be laid. The female arrives at the rookery and at nightfall begins her slow crawl up the beach. In many instances she returns to nest on the same beach where she herself hatched. She must move high enough up the beach so that water will not flood her nest. Once she is above the high-tide level, she digs a deep hole and lays 100 to 110 eggs, carefully covering them with sand and then making the long journey back to the water. The eggs contained in one nest are called a *clutch*. The female may repeat this process, laying as many as two to three clutches.

Left to develop in the warm sand, the baby turtles will not hatch for two to three months. During this time the eggs are easy prey for a variety of land predators. When they finally hatch, the young turtles must dig their way out of the sand and make a dash for the sea. Birds soar over the beach waiting for an easy meal. If the eggs hatch at night, the darkness may provide some cover, but even so, many of the turtles will never make it to the water. Even if they do reach the water, they still must avoid a large variety of marine predators. Their chances for survival are not good. Of the 100 eggs in a nest, only two will survive their first year of life.

Once they reach adulthood, sea turtles have few enemies. Humans have the greatest overall impact on sea turtle populations. Most rookeries are long stretches of wide, sandy beach—areas that are also popular with resort developers. Hotels and resorts, which are generally built near the high-tide line, greatly reduce the areas turtles can use for nesting. Native Central and South American people prize the flesh of sea turtles, and consider the eggs a delicacy. Fishing nets capture and drown large numbers of turtles every year. Discarded plastic bags, which resemble jellyfish when floating in the water, are mistakenly eaten by sea turtles, causing sickness or death. The large number of human impacts, combined with the low survival rate among baby sea turtles, has pushed these graceful creatures toward extinction.

Scientists have made many recommendations to help limit human impacts on the animals. Sea turtle farms now grow animals that can be released into the wild, and regulations limit the catch of adult turtles and eggs. In some countries, resort and hotel development has been restricted on beaches that sea turtles use as rookeries. Fishing nets have been changed to limit the number of turtles killed. With luck, these recommendations may help the sea turtle avoid extinction.

Sea turtles are mysterious animals. We know very little about their lives in the open ocean. We are fascinated as they return to nest in the same islands where they hatched. There is so much about them we do not know! What we do know is quite shocking. The numbers of almost all species of sea turtles continue to decrease every year. Unless we take the steps scientists recommend, the sea turtle will continue to fight a losing battle with extinction.

INDEX

PHOTO RESEARCH
Jim Rothaus / James R. Rothaus & Associates

PHOTO EDITOR
Robert A. Honey / Seattle

PHOTO CREDITS
INNERSPACE VISIONS / Doug Perrine:
front cover,11,17,21,31
Norbert Wu: 2,14,18,22,24,27,28
Marty Snyderman: 4
Anne Heimann: 7,8,13

Text copyright © 1996 by The Child's World, Inc.
All rights reserved. No part of this book may be reproduced
or utilized in any form or by any means without written
permission from the Publisher.
Printed in the United States of America.

Library of Congress Cataloging-in-Publication Data
Patton, Don.
Sea turtles / Don Patton.
p. cm.
Includes index.
ISBN 1-56766-188-2
(hardcover, reinforced library binding : alk. paper)
1. Sea turtles – Juvenile literature
[1. Sea turtles.] I. Title.
QL666.C536P38 1995   95-7858
597.92 – dc20   CIP
                                                 AC